A Butterfly Grows

A Butterfly Grows

by Stephen Swinburne

Green Light Readers

sandpiper

Houghton Mifflin Harcourt

Boston   New York   2009

Can you see me
on the plant?

I am a little caterpillar!
I grew in an egg.
Then I hatched!

Wind fills the
air. I hang on to
a branch so
I don't fall.

Rain falls. It plips and plops.
I need to drink water.
I drink the small drops.

This plant is my food. I need food so I can grow.

I eat this plant for lunch.
Chomp, chomp!
Crunch, munch!

I eat and grow,
eat and grow.
Now I am big!
My skin is snug.

I look for a spot to rest.
Soon I will shed my skin.

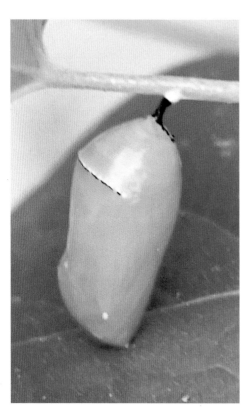

At last I am a chrysalis.
I'm an inch long.
Then in ten days,
out I come!

Look at me now!
I am an insect.
I have six legs.

My wings help me fly.
Watch me fly!

I like to fly with all my friends.
Wings help us play.
Wings help us to go find
plants for food.

Watch me eat now!
I sip and sip.

I am a butterfly!
I'm a beautiful butterfly!

What Do You Think?

- How does the caterpillar change in this story?

- Why does the caterpillar eat so much?

- Why do you think the author has the butterfly tell its own story?

- Imagine that you are a caterpillar or a butterfly for a day. Write about what you do.

Meet the Author/Photographer

Stephen Swinburne

loves nature—especially butterflies! He
planted a garden at his house filled with
flowers that butterflies like. He took many
of the pictures for *A Butterfly Grows*
in his garden. He hopes you enjoy
learning about butterflies!